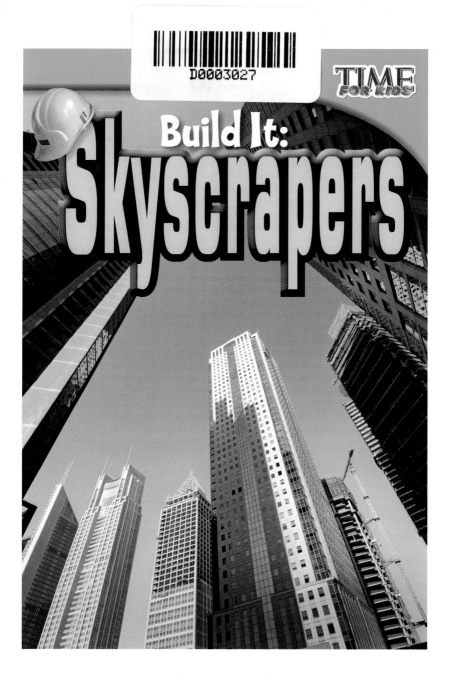

Build It:
Skyscrapers

TIME
FOR KIDS!

Madison Spielman

Consultant

Timothy Rasinski, Ph.D.
Kent State University

Publishing Credits

Dona Herweck Rice, *Editor-in-Chief*
Robin Erickson, *Production Director*
Lee Aucoin, *Creative Director*
Conni Medina, M.A.Ed., *Editorial Director*
Jamey Acosta, *Editor*
Stephanie Reid, *Photo Editor*
Rachelle Cracchiolo, M.S.Ed., *Publisher*

Based on writing from *TIME For Kids.*

Teacher Created Materials

5301 Oceanus Drive
Huntington Beach, CA 92649-1030
http://www.tcmpub.com

ISBN 978-1-4333-3620-1

© 2012 by Teacher Created Materials, Inc.
Made in China
Nordica.012018.CA21701270

Table of Contents

Room for Millions

Millions of people live and work in the world's biggest cities.

Is there enough room for them? Where do they live? Where do they work?

Long ago, big cities started to become too crowded. People had to find a way to make room for everyone. Since they had no more room to build *out,* they decided to build *up* instead.

Elevators

At first they could not build very high. How would people climb all of those stairs? Then the **elevator** was invented. People could easily get to the top of tall buildings.

That is how the first
skyscrapers came to be.

What Is a Skyscraper?

A skyscraper is a building that seems to scrape the sky. You must look up, up, up to see the top.

Skyscrapers must be very strong to go that high. Long ago, people did not know how to build such strong buildings. Now they know how.

Building Skyscrapers

First, machines dig a large, deep hole.

A structure of steel and **concrete** is then built in the hole. This is the **base**.

In order to be sturdy, a skyscraper must have a wide, strong base.

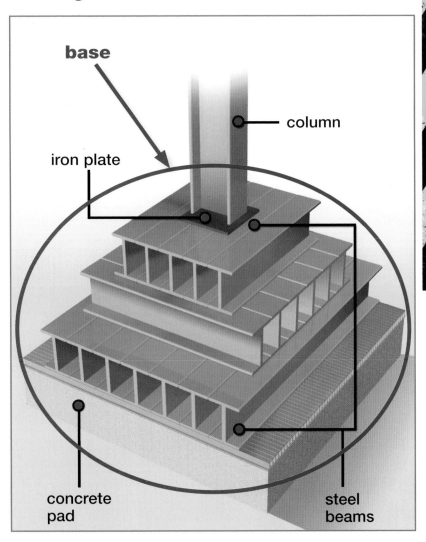

base

column

iron plate

concrete pad

steel beams

The base will help to hold the skyscraper and keep it in place.

Next, tall steel **beams** are added straight up from the base. They hold the weight of the skyscraper. The rest of the building will be attached to the beams.

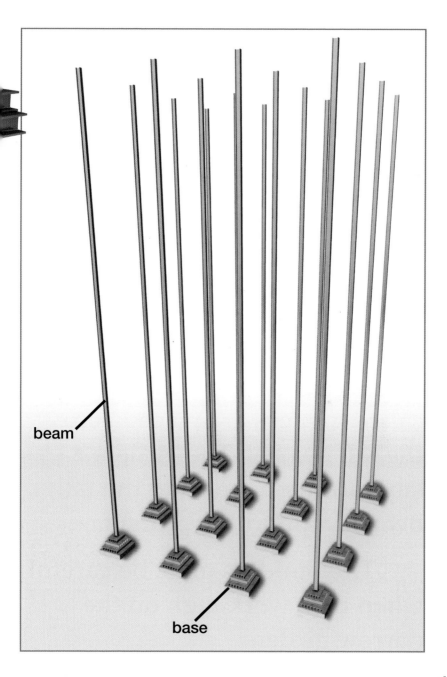

beam

base

The next step is to add the floors. First, more steel beams called **girders** are placed across the tall beams. The girders support the floors, and the tall beams support the girders.

The builders must be careful when they work high on the narrow girders!

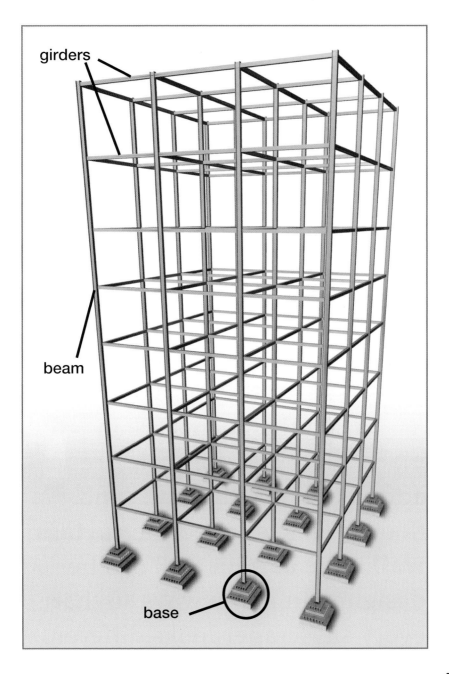

girders

beam

base

19

CONSTRUCTION ZONE

When the beams are in place, glass and concrete are added to make the walls and floors. This is called the **curtain wall**. The curtain wall can be designed in many ways so that every skyscraper looks different.

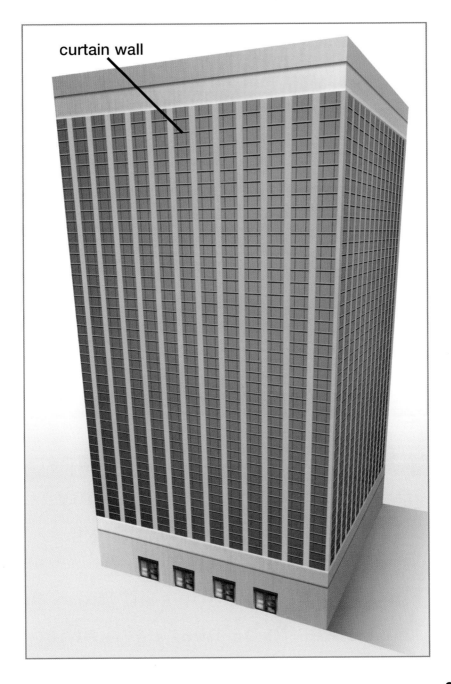

curtain wall

What Is Inside a Skyscraper?

Most of the time, skyscrapers are where people work. Many different companies can have offices in one skyscraper. The skyscraper allows all the companies to be near each other in one crowded city.

But people can live in skyscrapers, too.

Families who live in skyscrapers share them with many other families. Each family has its own home inside the skyscraper.

If you lived in a skyscraper, you might live on the 10th floor and your best friend might live on the 23rd floor. But you are still in the same building!

The Tallest Skyscrapers

Just how tall can a skyscraper be? There is no telling. People are always trying to build a skyscraper that is taller than the one before.

Some of the World's Tallest Skyscrapers

1,450 ft.	1,483 ft.	1,587 ft.	1,613 ft.	2,715 ft.
Sears Tower	**Petronas Towers**	**International Commercial Center**	**World Financial Center**	**Burj Khalifa**
Chicago	Malaysia	Hong Kong	Shanghai	Dubai

Sears Tower

Petronas Towers

When the Empire State Building in New York City was built, people thought that it was as tall as a building could go. Now, the Sears Tower in Chicago and the Petronas Towers in Malaysia are much taller.

Glossary

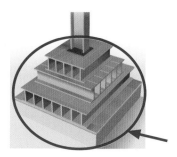

base

beams

concrete

curtain wall

elevator

girders

skyscrapers